I0012665

CODE ALCHEM.

TRANSFORMING YOUR CODE INTO GOLD

OLIVER LUCAS JR

PREFACE

The journey of a software developer is one of continuous learning and refinement. From the initial spark of an idea to the final polished product, code undergoes a transformation, evolving from raw concept to tangible solution. "Code Alchemy: Transforming Your Code into Gold" is a guide for this journey, offering a framework for understanding and mastering the art of code transformation. This book explores the principles and practices that empower developers to write cleaner, more maintainable code, ultimately creating software that is both functional and elegant.

This book is written for developers of all levels, from those just beginning their coding adventures to seasoned professionals seeking to refine their craft. Whether you're working on personal projects, contributing to open source, or developing enterprise-level applications, the techniques and principles presented here will provide you with valuable insights and practical tools to elevate your code. You will learn to identify areas for improvement, apply proven refactoring techniques, write effective tests, utilize design patterns wisely, and cultivate a culture of continuous improvement within your team. By the end of this book, you will not only write code that works, but code that is a pleasure to work with, both now and in the future.

My own journey as a developer has been deeply influenced by the pursuit of clean, maintainable code. I've learned that the true value of software lies not just in its functionality, but in its ability to adapt and evolve over time. This book is a culmination of those lessons, a distillation of the principles and practices that I've found most effective in transforming raw code into polished, valuable solutions.

TABLE OF CONTENTS

Chapter 5

Chapter 6

Chapter 7

Chapter 8

8.1 Leveraging IDEs: Utilizing Refactoring Features and Code Analysis Tools

8.2 Version Control Systems: Tracking Changes and Experimenting Safely

8.3 Continuous Integration and Continuous Delivery: Automating the Refactoring Process

Chapter 9

9.1 Analyzing a Real-World Codebase: Identifying Areas for Improvement

9.2 Applying Refactoring Techniques: Step-by-Step Transformation

9.3 Measuring the Impact: Evaluating the Benefits of Refactoring

Chapter 10

10.1 Building a Sustainable Codebase: Cultivating a Culture of Continuous Improvement

10.2 The Value of Refactoring: Investing in the Future of Your Software

10.3 Becoming a Code Alchemist: Mastering the Art of Transformation

Chapter 1

The Alchemist's Mindset

1.1 The Seeds of Transformation: Cultivating a Growth Mindset for Code Improvement

Embracing Continuous Learning: The Foundation of a Growth Mindset

A growth mindset is the belief that abilities and intelligence can be developed through dedication and hard work.[1] In the realm of coding, this translates to a willingness to embrace challenges, learn from mistakes, and seek out new knowledge. It's about viewing setbacks as opportunities for growth rather than personal failures. By cultivating a growth mindset, developers can unlock their full potential and transform their code into something truly remarkable.

The Power of Deliberate Practice: Transforming Effort into Mastery

Deliberate practice is a technique that involves focused effort and feedback to improve skills. It's about identifying areas for improvement, setting specific goals, and practicing consistently with the intention of getting better. Whether it's mastering a new programming language, learning a new design pattern, or refining coding techniques, deliberate practice is key to achieving mastery and transforming code into gold.

Celebrating Growth and Embracing Challenges: Nurturing a Positive Coding Culture

A positive and supportive environment can foster a growth mindset and encourage continuous improvement. Celebrating successes, both big and small, reinforces the value of effort and progress. Additionally, creating a culture that embraces challenges and encourages experimentation allows developers to step outside their comfort zones and explore new possibilities. By nurturing a positive coding culture, organizations can unlock the full potential of their developers and drive innovation.

1.2 The Alchemist's Tools: Essential Techniques for Code Analysis and Understanding

The Debugger: Unraveling the Mysteries of Execution

The debugger is an indispensable tool for understanding how code behaves at runtime. It allows developers to step through code line by line, inspect variables, and identify the root cause of unexpected behavior. By mastering the art of debugging, developers can quickly pinpoint errors, understand complex logic, and gain a deeper understanding of their code's inner workings.

Static Analysis: Unveiling Hidden Flaws and Potential Pitfalls

Static analysis tools examine code without executing it, identifying potential issues such as bugs, security vulnerabilities, and code smells. These tools can help developers catch problems early in the development cycle, improving code quality and reducing the risk of costly errors. By leveraging static analysis, developers can gain valuable insights into their code's structure, identify areas for improvement, and write more robust and maintainable software.

Code Reviews: The Power of Collective Wisdom

Code reviews involve having other developers examine code for potential issues and provide feedback. This collaborative process not only helps to improve code quality but also promotes knowledge sharing and fosters a culture of continuous learning. By actively participating in code reviews and providing constructive feedback, developers can sharpen their analytical skills, gain new perspectives, and elevate the overall quality of their work.

1.3 The First Spark: Recognizing the Need for Refactoring

Code Smells: Identifying Signs of Decaying Code

Code smells are indicators that the code may have underlying design problems. They are often subtle, but experienced developers can recognize them as signs that refactoring is necessary. Common code smells include:

Duplicate Code: Identical or very similar code blocks appearing in multiple places.

Long Methods: Methods that are excessively long and difficult to understand.

Large Classes: Classes that have too many responsibilities and are overly complex.

Primitive Obsession: Overuse of primitive data types instead of creating meaningful abstractions.

Switch Statements: Large switch statements that can become difficult to maintain and extend.

Technical Debt: Paying the Price of Quick Fixes

Technical debt is the accumulation of shortcuts and workarounds that were taken during development to meet deadlines or reduce initial effort. While these shortcuts may seem harmless initially, they can lead to significant problems down the line, such as increased maintenance costs, reduced flexibility, and increased risk of bugs. Recognizing and addressing technical debt through refactoring is crucial for long-term software sustainability.

Business Requirements: Adapting to Evolving Needs

As business requirements evolve, the software must also adapt. Refactoring is essential to ensure that the codebase remains flexible and can accommodate new features, changes in functionality, and evolving user needs. By proactively refactoring the code, developers can make future changes more quickly and efficiently, reducing the risk of introducing new bugs and improving the overall maintainability of the software.

Chapter 2

The Art of Decomposition

2.1 Breaking Down the Colossus: Deconstructing Complex Systems into Manageable Parts

The Power of Modularity: Building Blocks of Software

Modularity is a fundamental principle in software engineering that involves breaking down complex systems into smaller, more manageable components.[1] These components, or modules, should be independent and self-contained, with well-defined interfaces that allow them to interact with other modules.[2] This approach simplifies the development process, improves code reusability, and makes it easier to understand, maintain, and modify the system.[3]

The Art of Abstraction: Simplifying Complexity Through Generalization

Abstraction is the process of identifying and focusing on the essential features of a system while ignoring the irrelevant details.[4] By abstracting away complexity, developers can create higher-level concepts that represent the core functionality of the system.[5] This makes the code more readable, maintainable, and easier to reason about.[6]

Separation of Concerns: Isolating Functionality for Better Organization

Separation of concerns is a design principle that suggests breaking down a system into distinct parts, each responsible for a specific aspect of the system's functionality.[7] This approach helps to prevent unintended interactions between different parts of the system and makes it easier to isolate and fix problems.[8] By adhering to the principle of separation of concerns, developers can create more modular, maintainable, and scalable software systems.

2.2 The Power of Abstraction: Creating Higher-Level Concepts to Simplify Code

Identifying Common Patterns: Recognizing Recurring Themes in Your Code

Abstraction involves identifying common patterns and behaviors within your code and encapsulating them into higher-level concepts. By recognizing these recurring themes, you can create abstractions that simplify the code, reduce redundancy, and improve its maintainability. For example, if you find yourself repeatedly performing a set of operations on different types of data, you can create an abstract class or interface to represent the common behavior and then implement specific concrete classes for each data type.

Creating Interfaces: Defining Contracts for Interaction

Interfaces define a set of rules or contracts for how objects should interact with each other. By creating interfaces, you can decouple the implementation details of objects from their usage. This makes the code more flexible and easier to change, as you can easily substitute different implementations of the same interface without affecting the rest of the system.

Leveraging Libraries and Frameworks: Building Upon Existing Abstractions

Modern software development relies heavily on libraries and frameworks, which provide pre-built abstractions for common tasks such as data storage, user interface management, and network communication. By leveraging these existing abstractions, you can significantly reduce the amount of code you need to write, improve the quality of your code, and accelerate the development process. However, it's essential to understand the underlying abstractions and use them effectively to avoid introducing unnecessary complexity.

2.3 Identifying Code Smells: Recognizing Patterns of Impurity

Just as a fine goldsmith meticulously examines an ore for traces of impurities, a skilled programmer must develop a keen eye for "code smells" – telltale signs that your code might not be as pure and elegant as it could be. These smells often hint at deeper design issues, potential performance bottlenecks, or increased maintenance costs.

Here are some common code smells to watch out for:

Long Methods: Methods that stretch on for dozens or even hundreds of lines are often a sign of trouble. Long methods can be difficult to understand, debug, and maintain. They often violate the Single Responsibility Principle, meaning they do too many things at once.

Large Classes: Classes that are bloated with too many fields, methods, and responsibilities become unwieldy. They can be difficult to test, reuse, and understand. Consider breaking them down into smaller, more focused classes.

God Classes: These are the behemoths of the code world, controlling and knowing too much about the system. They often violate the Law of Demeter ("Don't Talk To Strangers"), leading to tight coupling and making it difficult to change any part of the system without affecting the God Class.

Primitive Obsession: Over-reliance on primitive data types (like integers and strings) can lead to inflexible and hard-to-maintain code. Consider creating custom data structures or value objects to encapsulate related information.

Switch Statements: Large switch statements can become difficult to maintain, especially as the number of cases grows. Consider using polymorphism or the Strategy pattern to achieve more flexible and maintainable code.

Duplicated Code: Code duplication is a major source of bugs and maintenance headaches. If you find yourself copying and pasting code blocks, consider refactoring to extract the common logic into a shared method or class.

Feature Envy: When a method in one class spends most of its time accessing data from another class, it might be "envious" of that other class. This often indicates that the method belongs in the other class.

Data Clumps: If you find the same set of variables appearing together frequently, it might be a sign that they should be grouped together into a separate class or data structure.

Shotgun Surgery: When you need to make a small change, you find yourself making small modifications in many different places. This often indicates that your code is tightly coupled and lacks cohesion.

Lazy Class: A class that does very little or has only a few methods might be an indication of unnecessary complexity. Consider merging it with another class or eliminating it entirely.

Recognizing the Patterns

Identifying code smells often requires a combination of experience, intuition, and code reviews.

Code Reviews: Regular code reviews provide an excellent opportunity to spot code smells and discuss potential improvements with your team.

Refactoring: The process of improving code without changing its external behavior can help you identify and eliminate code smells.

Automated Tools: Some tools can help you identify potential code smells, such as static analysis tools and code metrics.

The Importance of Purity

Just as goldsmiths strive to purify gold to its purest form, programmers should strive to eliminate code smells and improve the quality of their code. By identifying and addressing these impurities, you can create more maintainable, robust, and elegant software systems.

This is just a starting point. The art of identifying code smells requires continuous learning and refinement. By developing a keen eye for these patterns, you'll be well on your way to crafting truly exceptional code.

I hope this continues the story of "Code Alchemy" effectively. Feel free to ask if you have any further questions or want to explore specific code smells in more detail.

Chapter 3

The Alchemy of Abstraction

3.1 Encapsulation: Hiding Complexity, Revealing Simplicity

In the alchemical pursuit of transforming base code into golden solutions, encapsulation is akin to crafting a protective vessel for your most precious elements. It's about bundling data (attributes) and the methods that operate on that data into a single unit (a class), and controlling access to the internal workings of that unit. This "hiding" of complexity is not about secrecy, but about managing interactions and preventing unintended consequences.

Think of a complex machine like an engine. You don't need to understand the intricate workings of the pistons, valves, and crankshaft to drive a car. You interact with the engine through a simplified interface: the accelerator, the ignition, and the gearshift. Encapsulation works similarly in code.

The Pillars of Encapsulation:

Data Hiding: This is the core principle. Internal data (instance variables or attributes) are declared as `private` (or similarly restricted in other languages). This prevents direct access from outside the class. Instead, access is controlled through public methods (getters and setters, or accessors and mutators).

Example: Imagine a `BankAccount` class. The `balance` attribute should be private. You wouldn't want any part of the program directly modifying the balance without going through proper checks (like ensuring sufficient funds for a withdrawal).

Abstraction: Encapsulation goes hand-in-hand with abstraction. By hiding the internal implementation details, you present a simplified view of the object to the outside world. Users of your class only need to know *what* the object does, not *how* it does it.

Example: A `withdraw(amount)` method on the `BankAccount` class abstracts away the complex logic of checking balances, deducting the amount, and potentially handling overdrafts. The user simply calls `withdraw(100)` and expects the balance to be updated accordingly.

Information Hiding: This closely relates to data hiding and emphasizes controlling access to the internal state of an object. This prevents external code from accidentally corrupting the data or putting the object into an invalid state.

Example: By making the `balance` private and providing a `deposit(amount)` method, you can ensure that only valid positive amounts can be added to the balance, preventing accidental negative balances.

Benefits of Encapsulation:

Modularity: Encapsulated code is more modular. Changes to the internal implementation of a class don't affect other parts of the system, as long as the public interface remains the same. This allows for easier maintenance and refactoring.

Maintainability: Because changes are localized, debugging and maintaining encapsulated code becomes much simpler. You can focus on the specific class without worrying about ripple effects throughout the application.

Flexibility: Encapsulation allows you to change the internal representation of data without affecting the code that uses the class. For example, you could change how the `balance` is stored (e.g., from an integer to a decimal) without breaking any code that uses the `BankAccount` class.

Reusability: Well-encapsulated classes are more reusable. They can be easily integrated into different parts of the application or even into other projects.

Security: By controlling access to data, encapsulation enhances the security of your code. You can implement validation rules and prevent unauthorized access or modification of sensitive information.

The Golden Vessel:

Encapsulation is not merely a technical detail; it's a fundamental principle of good software design. It's the alchemist's vessel, containing and protecting the valuable transformations within. By carefully managing access and hiding complexity, you create code that is more robust, maintainable, and ultimately, more valuable. It allows you to build complex systems from manageable, self-contained components, transforming the raw ore of code into refined, golden solutions.

This continues our "Code Alchemy" narrative. Let me know if you'd like to explore other related concepts like inheritance or polymorphism.

3.2 Polymorphism: Adapting to Change with Grace

In the realm of alchemy, the ability to transmute one substance into another is the ultimate goal. In the world of code, polymorphism offers a similar kind of transformation, allowing objects of different classes to be treated as objects of a common type. This adaptability is crucial for creating flexible, extensible, and maintainable software.

The word "polymorphism" comes from the Greek words "poly" (many) and "morph" (forms). In programming, it means "many forms" or "many shapes." It's the ability of an object to take on many forms.

Two Main Types of Polymorphism:

Compile-Time Polymorphism (Static Polymorphism or Method Overloading): This type of polymorphism is resolved at compile time. It's achieved through method overloading, where you define multiple methods with the same name but different parameters (number, type, or order). The compiler determines which method to call based on the arguments provided.

Example: Imagine a `Calculator` class with multiple `add()` methods:

Java

```
class Calculator {
    int add(int a, int b) { return a + b; }
    double add(double a, double b) { return a + b; }
    String add(String a, String b) { return a + b; }
}
```

When you call `add(2, 3)`, the compiler knows to use the `int add(int a, int b)` method. When you call `add(2.5, 3.7)`, it uses the `double add(double a, double b)` method.

Runtime Polymorphism (Dynamic Polymorphism or Method Overriding): This type of polymorphism is resolved at runtime. It's achieved through method overriding, which occurs when a subclass provides a specific implementation for a method that is already defined in its superclass. The[1] actual method called is determined at runtime based on the object's actual type.

Example: Consider a Shape class with a draw() method:
Java

```java
class Shape {
    void draw() { System.out.println("Drawing a generic shape"); }
}

class Circle extends Shape {
    @Override
    void draw() { System.out.println("Drawing a circle"); }
}

class Square extends Shape {
    @Override
    void draw() { System.out.println("Drawing a square"); }
}
```

If you have a Shape reference that points to a Circle object:

Java

```java
Shape myShape = new Circle();
myShape.draw(); // Output: Drawing a circle
```

Even though myShape is declared as a Shape, the draw() method of the Circle class is called at runtime. This is dynamic polymorphism in action.

Benefits of Polymorphism:

Extensibility: Polymorphism makes it easy to add new types of objects to your system without modifying existing code. You can create new subclasses and override methods as needed.

Code Reusability: By using a common interface or superclass, you can write code that works with objects of different types, promoting code reuse.

Flexibility: Polymorphism allows you to write more generic and flexible code. You can write methods that accept objects of a superclass and work correctly with any of its subclasses.

Maintainability: Polymorphism makes it easier to maintain and modify code. Changes to one part of the system are less likely to affect other parts.

The Alchemist's Transmutation:

Polymorphism is the alchemist's ability to transform code into different forms, adapting to various situations with grace and efficiency. It allows you to write code that is more flexible, extensible, and easier to maintain. By embracing polymorphism, you can create software that gracefully handles change and evolves over time, truly transforming base code into golden solutions.

This concludes our exploration of Polymorphism in the context of Code Alchemy. We've covered the core principles of Object-Oriented Programming (Encapsulation, Inheritance - implicitly through overriding, and Polymorphism). Let me know if you would like to explore other concepts or revisit any of these in more detail.

3.3 Inheritance: Building Upon Existing Foundations

In the alchemical tradition, the knowledge and wisdom of past masters are essential for making new discoveries. Similarly, in software development, inheritance allows us to build upon existing code, creating new classes that inherit the properties and behaviors of existing ones. This promotes code reuse, reduces redundancy, and fosters a hierarchical organization of classes.

Inheritance establishes an "is-a" relationship between classes. A subclass (or derived class) *is a* specialized version of its superclass (or base class). For example, a `Car` *is a* `Vehicle`, a `Dog` *is an* `Animal`.

Key Concepts of Inheritance:

Superclass (Base Class or Parent Class): The class whose properties and behaviors are inherited by other classes.

Subclass (Derived Class or Child Class): The class that inherits properties and behaviors from a superclass.

Inheritance Relationship: The relationship between a superclass and its subclasses, denoted by "is-a."

Code Reuse: Subclasses inherit the fields (attributes) and methods of their superclass, avoiding the need to rewrite the same code.

Extensibility: Subclasses can add new fields and methods, or override existing methods, to extend or modify the behavior of the superclass.

How Inheritance Works:

When a subclass inherits from a superclass, it automatically gains access to all the non-private members (fields and methods) of the superclass. The subclass can then:

Use the inherited members as they are: The subclass can directly use the fields and methods inherited from the superclass without any modifications.

Add new members: The subclass can define its own fields and methods that are specific to its functionality.

Override existing methods: The subclass can provide a new implementation for a method that is already defined in the superclass. This is known as method overriding and is a key aspect of polymorphism (which we discussed previously).

Example:

Let's consider a simple example with Animal as the superclass and Dog as the subclass:

```java
Java
class Animal {
   String name;

   Animal(String name) {
      this.name = name;
   }

   void eat() {
      System.out.println(name + " is eating.");
   }

   void makeSound() {
      System.out.println(name + " makes a generic sound.");
   }
}

class Dog extends Animal {
   String breed;

   Dog(String name, String breed) {
      super(name); // Call the superclass constructor
      this.breed = breed;
```

```java
    }

    @Override
    void makeSound() {
            System.out.println(name + " barks."); // Override the
makeSound method
    }

    void wagTail() {
       System.out.println(name + " wags its tail.");
    }
}

public class Main {
    public static void main(String[] args) {
       Dog myDog = new Dog("Buddy", "Golden Retriever");
        myDog.eat();      // Output: Buddy is eating. (Inherited from
Animal)
        myDog.makeSound();// Output: Buddy barks. (Overridden in
Dog)
        myDog.wagTail();  // Output: Buddy wags its tail. (Specific to
Dog)

       Animal myAnimal = new Animal("Generic Animal");
        myAnimal.makeSound();// Output: Generic Animal makes a
generic sound.
    }
}
```

Benefits of Inheritance:

Code Reusability: Avoids redundant code by reusing existing
code from superclasses.

Improved Organization: Creates a hierarchical structure of classes, making the code more organized and easier to understand.

Extensibility: Allows you to easily extend the functionality of existing classes without modifying them directly.

Maintainability: Changes to the superclass automatically affect all its subclasses, simplifying maintenance.

The Alchemist's Legacy:

Inheritance is like inheriting the wisdom and tools of previous alchemists. It allows us to build upon the foundations laid by others, creating more complex and sophisticated solutions. By using inheritance effectively, we can create well-structured, maintainable, and extensible code that truly transforms raw code into refined and valuable solutions.

This concludes our discussion of Inheritance within the context of Code Alchemy. We've now covered the core pillars of Object-Oriented Programming: Encapsulation, Inheritance, and Polymorphism. Let me know if you would like to explore any other related concepts or revisit any of these in more detail.

Chapter 4

The Elixir of Clean Code

4.1 Meaningful Naming: Choosing Names that Speak for Themselves

In the alchemical pursuit of crafting code that transcends mere functionality and achieves true elegance, the art of naming is paramount. Just as an alchemist carefully labels each ingredient and apparatus, a programmer must meticulously choose names for variables, functions, classes, and other code elements. Meaningful names act as signposts, guiding readers through the code and illuminating its purpose.

Meaningful naming is not just about avoiding cryptic abbreviations or single-letter variables. It's about choosing names that clearly and unambiguously convey the *intent* and *purpose* of the code element. Names should be self-documenting, reducing the need for excessive comments and making the code easier to understand and maintain.

Principles of Meaningful Naming:

Use Descriptive Names: Choose names that clearly describe what the variable, function, or class represents. Avoid vague or generic names like `data`, `value`, or `temp`.

Bad: `int d;`

Good: `int daysSinceLastLogin;`

Be Consistent: Use a consistent naming convention throughout your codebase. This makes it easier to recognize different types of elements and understand their purpose. Common conventions include:

Camel Case: `firstName`, `calculateTotalPrice` (used for variables and methods in many languages)

Pascal Case: `CustomerOrder`, `DatabaseConnection` (used for classes in many languages)

Snake Case: `first_name`, `calculate_total_price` (used in Python and other languages)

UPPER_SNAKE_CASE: `MAX_VALUE`, `DATABASE_URL` (used for constants)

Use Pronounceable Names: Choose names that are easy to pronounce. This makes it easier to discuss the code with others and reduces the risk of miscommunication.

Bad: `int nmbrOfCstms;`

Good: `int numberOfCustomers;`

Avoid Abbreviations (Unless Widely Understood): Avoid abbreviations unless they are widely understood within the context of your project or domain. Over-abbreviation can make the code cryptic and difficult to understand.

Bad: `int custId;` (Unless in a context where `cust` is universally understood)

Good: `int customerId;`

Use Searchable Names: Choose names that are easy to search for in your codebase. This makes it easier to find and modify specific parts of the code.

Boolean Variables Should Be Clear: Boolean variables should have names that clearly indicate their true/false meaning.

Bad: `boolean flag;`

Good: `boolean isUserLoggedIn;` or `boolean hasPermission;`

Method Names Should Describe Actions: Method names should clearly describe the action they perform. Use verbs to start method names.

Bad: `void data();`

Good: `void loadUserData();` or `void calculateTotal();`

Class Names Should Be Nouns: Class names should be nouns or noun phrases that describe the objects they represent.

Bad: `class ManageData;`

Good: `class DataManager;` or `class Customer;`

Be Mindful of Scope: The length of a name should be proportional to its scope. Short names are acceptable for local variables with limited scope, while longer, more descriptive names are needed for global variables or class members.

The Alchemist's Inscription:

Meaningful naming is like carefully inscribing each component of your alchemical creation. Clear and descriptive names illuminate the purpose and function of each element, making the entire creation more understandable and manageable. By choosing names that speak for themselves, you transform code from a cryptic collection of symbols into a clear and expressive language, facilitating collaboration, maintenance, and the overall success of your software projects. This practice is essential for transforming base code into truly golden solutions.

4.2   Functions   with   Purpose: Single Responsibility and Minimal Arguments

In the alchemical process of refining code, functions are the crucibles where transformations take place. To ensure these transformations are precise and predictable, each function should adhere to the principles of single responsibility and minimize the number of arguments it receives. This leads to code that is more modular, testable, and easier to understand.

Single Responsibility Principle (SRP) for Functions:

Just as each tool in an alchemist's workshop has a specific purpose, each function in your code should have one, and only one, well-defined responsibility. This principle, known as the Single Responsibility Principle (SRP), is crucial for creating maintainable and robust code.

A function with a single responsibility is easier to understand, test, and reuse. If a function tries to do too many things, it becomes complex, difficult to debug, and prone to unintended side effects.

Benefits of SRP for Functions:

Improved Readability: Functions with a single purpose are easier to understand because their functionality is clearly defined.

Introduce Parameter Objects: Create a new class to hold related parameters.

Reduce Coupling: Avoid passing objects that are only used to access a single method or property. Consider passing only the necessary data instead.

Example of Reducing Arguments:

Before:

Java

```java
void drawRectangle(int x, int y, int width, int height, String color) {
/* ... */ }
```

After:

Java

```java
class Rectangle {
    int x;
    int y;
    int width;
    int height;
    String color;

    // ... constructor and other methods
}

void drawRectangle(Rectangle rectangle) { /* ... */ }
```

By encapsulating the rectangle's properties into a Rectangle object, we've reduced the number of arguments to the drawRectangle function to just one.

The Alchemist's Precision:

By adhering to the principles of single responsibility and minimal arguments, you create functions that are precise and predictable, like the carefully measured ingredients in an alchemist's formula. This leads to code that is more modular, testable, and easier to understand, transforming raw code into refined and valuable solutions.

4.3 Comments That Enlighten: Explaining "Why," Not "What"

In the alchemical pursuit of creating code that is not only functional but also understandable, comments play a crucial role. However, the true value of a comment lies not in simply restating what the code already clearly expresses, but in illuminating the *reasoning* behind the code – the "why" rather than the "what."

The Problem with Redundant Comments:

Many comments simply reiterate the obvious. For example:

```java
Java
int x = 5; // Assign 5 to x
```

This comment is redundant. The code itself clearly states that 5 is being assigned to x. Such comments clutter the code and add no real value. In fact, they can become a maintenance burden. If the code changes and the comment is not updated, it becomes misleading.

Focus on "Why," Not "What":

Effective comments explain the *intent*, the *reasoning*, the *context*, or the *constraints* behind the code. They answer questions like:

Why was this particular approach chosen?

What are the edge cases or special considerations?

What are the limitations or trade-offs?

What is the high-level purpose of this code section?

Examples of Effective Comments:

Explaining a non-obvious algorithm:

Java

```
// Use the Sieve of Eratosthenes algorithm to find all prime
numbers up to n.
// This is more efficient than trial division for larger values of n.
// See: https://en.wikipedia.org/wiki/Sieve_of_Eratosthenes
for (int i = 2; i * i <= n; i++) {
    // ...
}
```

Explaining a workaround or a hack:

Java

```
// Workaround for a bug in the legacy database driver that doesn't
handle null dates correctly.
// This will be removed once the driver is updated.
if (date == null) {
    date = new Date(0); // Set to epoch time as a temporary
solution.
}
```

Explaining design decisions:

Java

```java
// Using a HashMap for caching because lookups are expected to
be frequent.
// A LinkedHashMap could be considered if insertion order needs
to be preserved.
private Map<String, User> userCache = new HashMap<>();
```

Explaining important business rules:

Java

```java
// Users with an "admin" role are exempt from the daily login limit.
if (user.getRole().equals("admin")) {
    return;
}
```

Documenting complex regular expressions:

Java

```java
// Matches email addresses according to RFC 5322.
// This is a complex expression, but it ensures robust email
validation.
private static final Pattern EMAIL_PATTERN = Pattern.compile(

"^[a-zA-Z0-9_+&*-]+(?:\\.[a-zA-Z0-9_+&*-]+)*@(?:[a-zA-Z0-9-]+\\.)
+[a-zA-Z]{2,7}$"
);
```

When to Comment (and When Not To):

Don't comment obvious code: Code should be self-documenting as much as possible through meaningful names and clear structure.

Do comment non-obvious code: Explain complex logic, algorithms, workarounds, or important design decisions.

Do comment to explain the "why": Focus on the reasoning behind the code, not just restating what it does.

Do keep comments up to date: Outdated comments are worse than no comments at all.

The Alchemist's Notes:

Effective comments are like the alchemist's meticulous notes, recording the rationale behind each experiment and observation. They provide valuable context and insight, making the code more understandable and maintainable for both the original author and others who may work with it in the future. By focusing on explaining "why," you transform comments from mere noise into valuable tools for understanding and refining your code.

Chapter 5

The Crucible of Testing

5.1 The Importance of Unit Tests: Building a Safety Net for Refactoring

In the alchemical pursuit of transforming code into more refined and valuable forms, refactoring is an essential process. It's akin to purifying a substance, removing impurities and improving its properties without changing its fundamental nature. However, refactoring can be risky. Without a safety net, changes can introduce unintended bugs or break existing functionality. This is where unit tests become invaluable.

What are Unit Tests?

Unit tests are automated tests that verify the behavior of small, isolated units of code, typically individual functions or methods. They focus on testing specific inputs and verifying the expected outputs. A good suite of unit tests provides confidence that changes to the code haven't broken anything.

Why are Unit Tests Important for Refactoring?

Regression Prevention: The primary benefit of unit tests during refactoring is preventing regressions. When you change the code, you run the unit tests. If any tests fail, it indicates that your changes have introduced a bug. This allows you to catch and fix problems early, before they make their way into production.

Confidence in Changes: Unit tests provide confidence to make changes. Knowing that you have a safety net of tests allows you to refactor more aggressively and improve the code without fear of breaking things.

Living Documentation: Unit tests serve as a form of living documentation. They demonstrate how the code is intended to be used and what its expected behavior is. This can be very helpful for developers who are new to the codebase or who are working on unfamiliar parts of the code.

Faster Feedback: Unit tests provide fast feedback. They run quickly, allowing you to get immediate feedback on your changes. This rapid feedback loop is essential for efficient refactoring.

Simplified Debugging: When a bug does occur, unit tests can help you pinpoint the source of the problem. If a specific test fails, it isolates the bug to the unit of code that the test covers.

Characteristics of Good Unit Tests:

Fast: Unit tests should run quickly so that developers can run them frequently.

Independent: Unit tests should be independent of each other. The outcome of one test should not affect the outcome of another.

Repeatable: Unit tests should produce the same results every time they are run, regardless of the environment.

Self-Validating: Unit tests should automatically determine whether they have passed or failed.

Thorough: Unit tests should cover all important code paths and edge cases.

Written Before or During Development (Test-Driven Development - TDD): Ideally, unit tests are written before or during the development of the code they test. This practice, known as Test-Driven Development (TDD), can lead to better design and more testable code.

Example:

Let's say you have a function that calculates the area of a rectangle:

Java
```
int calculateArea(int width, int height) {
    return width * height;
}
```

A unit test for this function might look like this (using JUnit):

Java
```
import org.junit.jupiter.api.Test;
import static org.junit.jupiter.api.Assertions.*;

public class RectangleTest {

    @Test
    void testCalculateArea() {
        assertEquals(12, calculateArea(3, 4));
        assertEquals(0, calculateArea(0, 5));
        assertEquals(25, calculateArea(5, 5));
    }

    int calculateArea(int width, int height) {
        return width * height;
    }
}
```

If you were to refactor the `calculateArea` function, you could run this test to ensure that your changes haven't broken its functionality.

The Alchemist's Safeguard:

Unit tests are the alchemist's safeguard, ensuring that the process of refinement doesn't inadvertently introduce impurities. They provide a safety net for refactoring, allowing you to make changes with confidence and transform code into more elegant and efficient forms. By embracing unit testing, you create more robust, maintainable, and ultimately, more valuable software.

5.2 Let's delve into the practice of Test-Driven Development (TDD):

In our ongoing analogy of Code Alchemy, TDD is akin to meticulously planning and documenting every step of an experiment *before* actually performing it. This approach, though seemingly counterintuitive at first, leads to more robust, well-designed, and easily maintainable code.

Test-Driven Development (TDD) is a software development process that emphasizes writing tests *before* writing the code that implements the functionality. It follows a short, iterative cycle known as "Red-Green-Refactor":

Red: Write a failing test. Before writing any code, you write a test that defines the desired behavior of a small piece of functionality. Because the code doesn't exist yet, the test will fail (hence "Red").

Green: Write the minimum amount of code to make the test pass. Once you have a failing test, you write the simplest code possible to make it pass (hence "Green"). The focus is on getting the test to pass, not on writing perfect or elegant code at this stage.

Refactor: Refactor the code to improve its design and structure, while ensuring that all tests still pass. Now that you have working code, you can focus on improving its quality without fear of breaking anything, as your tests act as a safety net.

The TDD Cycle in Detail:

Write a Failing Test (Red):

Start by clearly defining the desired behavior of the code you are about to write.

Write a small, focused test that specifically targets that behavior.

Run the test. It should fail because the code to implement the behavior doesn't exist yet. This failing test confirms that the test itself is working correctly.

Write the Minimum Code to Pass the Test (Green):

Write the simplest possible code that will make the test pass.

Don't worry about perfect design or elegance at this stage. The goal is simply to get the test to pass.

Run the test again. It should now pass.

Refactor (Refactor):

Now that you have working code and a passing test, you can refactor the code to improve its design, structure, and readability.

Run all tests after each refactoring step to ensure that you haven't introduced any regressions.

Benefits of TDD:

Improved Design: TDD forces you to think about the design of your code before you write it. This leads to more modular, cohesive, and testable code.

Reduced Bugs: By writing tests first, you catch bugs earlier in the development process, when they are easier and cheaper to fix.

Increased Confidence: TDD gives you confidence to make changes to your code, knowing that your tests will catch any regressions.

Living Documentation: Tests serve as a form of living documentation, demonstrating how the code is intended to be used.

Faster Feedback: TDD provides rapid feedback on your changes, allowing you to iterate quickly and efficiently.

Clearer Requirements: The process of writing tests forces you to clarify the requirements of the code you are writing.

Example:

Let's say you want to write a function that adds two numbers:

Red: Write a test:

Java

```java
import org.junit.jupiter.api.Test;
import static org.junit.jupiter.api.Assertions.*;

public class CalculatorTest {
    @Test
    void testAddTwoNumbers() {
        assertEquals(5, add(2, 3));
    }

    int add(int a, int b){
        return 0; //Stub to make the test compile.
    }
}
```

This test will fail because the add function currently returns 0.

Green: Write the minimum code to pass the test:

Java

```
int add(int a, int b){
    return a + b;
}
```

Now the test will pass.

Refactor: In this simple example, there's not much to refactor. However, in more complex scenarios, you would now refactor the code to improve its design, while ensuring that the test still passes.

The Alchemist's Blueprint:

TDD is the alchemist's blueprint, meticulously outlining each step of the transformation process before it begins. This disciplined approach leads to code that is more robust, reliable, and easier to maintain, ultimately transforming raw code into refined and valuable solutions. By writing tests first, you gain a deeper understanding of the problem you are solving and create code that is more likely to meet the desired requirements.

5.3 Refactoring with Confidence: Using Tests to Guide Change

In the realm of Code Alchemy, refactoring is the process of purifying and refining existing code without changing its external behavior. It's about improving the internal structure, readability, and maintainability of the code, making it more elegant and efficient. However, refactoring can be risky if not done carefully. This is where a robust suite of tests becomes essential, acting as a safety net and providing confidence to make changes.

What is Refactoring?

Refactoring is the process of improving the internal structure of existing code while preserving its external behavior. It's not about adding new features or fixing bugs (though it can sometimes uncover them). Instead, it's about making the code cleaner, more readable, more maintainable, and easier to understand.

Why Refactor?

Improve Readability: Refactored code is easier to understand, making it easier for developers to work with and maintain.

Reduce Complexity: Refactoring can simplify complex code, making it less prone to errors and easier to modify.

Improve Maintainability: Cleaner code is easier to maintain and modify in the future.

Improve Performance (Sometimes): While the primary goal of refactoring is not performance improvement, it can sometimes lead to performance gains by optimizing algorithms or data structures.

Improve Design: Refactoring can help improve the overall design of the code, making it more modular, cohesive, and extensible.

The Importance of Tests in Refactoring:

A comprehensive suite of unit tests is absolutely crucial for safe and confident refactoring. Tests act as a safety net, ensuring that changes made during refactoring do not introduce new bugs or break existing functionality.

How Tests Guide Refactoring:

Establish a Baseline: Before starting any refactoring, ensure you have a comprehensive suite of passing unit tests. These tests establish a baseline of expected behavior.

Make Small Changes: Refactor in small, incremental steps. This makes it easier to track changes and identify any problems that may arise.

Run Tests Frequently: After each small change, run the unit tests to ensure that you haven't broken anything. If a test fails, you know that your change has introduced a bug and you can revert or fix it immediately.

Refactor with Confidence: With a solid suite of tests, you can refactor with confidence, knowing that you have a safety net to catch any regressions.

Common Refactoring Techniques:

Extract Method: Extracting a block of code into a separate method to improve readability and reduce code duplication.

Rename Method/Variable: Giving methods and variables more descriptive names to improve understanding.

Move Method/Field: Moving methods or fields to a more appropriate class to improve cohesion and reduce coupling.

Extract Class: Creating a new class to encapsulate related data and behavior.

Inline Method: Replacing a method call with the method's body.

Replace Temp with Query: Replacing a temporary variable with a method call that calculates the value.

Example:

Let's say you have a method that calculates the price of an order:

Java
```
double calculateOrderPrice(List<OrderItem> items) {
```

```java
    double totalPrice = 0;
    for (OrderItem item : items) {
        totalPrice += item.getPrice() * item.getQuantity();
    }
    if (totalPrice > 100) {
        totalPrice *= 0.9; // 10% discount for orders over $100
    }
    return totalPrice;
}
```

You could refactor this method to extract the discount logic into a separate method:

Java
```java
double calculateOrderPrice(List<OrderItem> items) {
    double totalPrice = calculateTotalWithoutDiscount(items);
    return applyDiscount(totalPrice);
}

private double calculateTotalWithoutDiscount(List<OrderItem> items) {
    double totalPrice = 0;
    for (OrderItem item : items) {
        totalPrice += item.getPrice() * item.getQuantity();
    }
    return totalPrice;
}

private double applyDiscount(double totalPrice) {
    if (totalPrice > 100) {
        totalPrice *= 0.9;
    }
    return totalPrice;
}
```

Before and after this refactoring, you would run your unit tests to ensure that the behavior of the `calculateOrderPrice` method has not changed.

The Alchemist's Refinement:

Refactoring, guided by a robust test suite, is the alchemist's process of refinement. It allows you to transform code into a more pure and valuable form, improving its quality without altering its essence. By using tests as a safety net, you can refactor with confidence, knowing that you are not introducing new problems but rather improving the overall quality of your codebase.

Chapter 6

The Philosopher's Stone: Design Patterns

6.1 Understanding Design Patterns: Timeless Solutions to Common Problems

In the alchemical pursuit of crafting elegant and efficient code, design patterns serve as time-tested formulas, offering proven solutions to recurring design challenges. They are not ready-made code snippets that you can simply copy and paste, but rather reusable solutions to common problems that arise during software development. They represent best practices and capture the experience of seasoned developers.

What are Design Patterns?

Design patterns are reusable solutions to commonly occurring problems in software design. They are templates or blueprints that can be adapted to solve similar problems in different contexts. They provide a common vocabulary for developers to communicate about design issues and solutions.

Key Characteristics of Design Patterns:

Problem: Each pattern describes a recurring problem in a specific context.

Solution: Each pattern provides a general solution to the problem, described in terms of objects and their relationships.

Context: Each pattern describes the context in which the solution is applicable.

Forces: Each pattern explains the forces or trade-offs that influence the solution.

Benefits of Using Design Patterns:

Proven Solutions: Design patterns represent best practices that have been proven effective over time.

Improved Communication: They provide a common vocabulary for developers to discuss design issues.

Increased Code Reusability: They promote code reuse by providing reusable solutions.

Improved Code Maintainability: They lead to more structured and understandable code.

Faster Development: They can speed up development by providing ready-made solutions to common problems.

Categories of Design Patterns:

Design patterns are typically categorized into three main groups:

Creational Patterns: These patterns deal with object creation mechanisms, trying to create objects in a manner suitable to the situation. Examples include:

Singleton:[1] Ensures that a class has only one instance and provides a global point of access to it.

Factory Method: Defines an interface for creating objects, but lets subclasses decide which class to instantiate.

Abstract Factory: Provides an interface for creating families of related or dependent objects without specifying their concrete classes.

Builder: Separates the construction of[2] a complex object from its representation so that the same construction process can create different representations.

Prototype:[3] Specifies the kinds of objects to create using a prototypical instance, and create new objects by copying this[4] prototype.

Structural Patterns: These patterns deal with the composition of classes or objects to form larger structures. Examples include:

Adapter: Converts the interface of a class into another interface clients expect. Adapter lets classes work together that couldn't otherwise because of incompatible interfaces.[5]

Composite: Composes objects into tree structures to represent part-whole hierarchies. Composite lets clients treat individual objects and compositions of objects uniformly.[6]

Decorator: Dynamically[7] adds responsibilities to an object. Decorators provide a flexible alternative to subclassing for extending functionality.

Facade: Provides a unified interface to a set of[8] interfaces in a subsystem. Facade defines a higher-level interface that makes the subsystem easier[9] to use.

Flyweight: Uses sharing to support large numbers of fine-grained objects efficiently.[10]

Proxy: Provides a surrogate or placeholder for another object to control access to it.

Behavioral Patterns: These patterns deal with algorithms and the assignment of responsibilities between objects. Examples include:

Chain of Responsibility: Avoids coupling the sender of a request to its receiver by giving multiple objects a chance to handle the request. Chain the receiving objects and pass the request along the chain until an object handles it.

Command: Encapsulates[11] a request as an object, thereby letting you parameterize clients with different requests, queue or log requests, and support undoable operations.[12]

Interpreter: Given a language, define a representation for its grammar along with an interpreter that uses the[13] representation to interpret sentences in the language.

Iterator: Provides[14] a way to access the elements of an aggregate object sequentially without exposing its underlying representation.

Mediator: Defines[15] an object that encapsulates how a set of objects interact. Mediator promotes loose coupling by keeping objects from referring to each other explicitly, and[16] it lets you vary their interaction independently.

Memento: Without violating encapsulation, capture and externalize an object's internal state so that the object[17] can be restored to this state later.[18]

Observer: Defines a one-to-many dependency between objects so that when one object changes state, all its dependents are notified and updated automatically.[19]

State: Allows an object to alter its behavior when its internal state changes. The object will appear to change its class.[20]

Strategy: Defines a family of algorithms, encapsulates each one, and makes them interchangeable. Strategy lets the algorithm vary independently from clients that use[21] it.

Template Method: Defines the skeleton of an algorithm in an operation, deferring some steps to subclasses. Template Method lets subclasses[22] redefine certain steps of an algorithm without changing the algorithm's structure.[23]

Visitor: Represents an operation to be performed on the elements of an object structure. Visitor lets you define a new operation without[24] changing the classes of the elements on which it operates.

The[25] Alchemist's Grimoire:

Design patterns are like the alchemist's grimoire, a collection of proven formulas and techniques for achieving specific transformations. By understanding and applying these patterns, you can create more robust, maintainable, and elegant code, transforming raw code into refined and valuable solutions. They provide a common language and a shared understanding of best practices, facilitating collaboration and improving the overall quality of software development.

6.2 Applying Design Patterns Effectively: Choosing the Right Tool for the Job

In our Code Alchemy analogy, design patterns are like the specialized tools in an alchemist's workshop. Each tool is designed for a specific purpose, and using the wrong tool can lead to ineffective results or even damage the creation. Similarly, applying design patterns effectively requires careful consideration of the context and choosing the right pattern to address the specific problem at hand.

Understanding the Context:

Before applying any design pattern, it's crucial to thoroughly understand the context of the problem you are trying to solve. This involves:

Identifying the Problem: Clearly define the problem you are facing. What are the specific challenges you are trying to address?

Understanding the Requirements: What are the functional and non-functional requirements of the system?

Analyzing the Constraints: What are the limitations or constraints that you need to consider (e.g., performance, memory, platform)?

Considering the Trade-offs: Each design pattern has its own set of trade-offs. It's important to understand these trade-offs and choose the pattern that best balances them in the given context.

Choosing the Right Pattern:

Once you have a clear understanding of the context, you can start considering which design pattern might be appropriate. Here are some guidelines:

Don't Force a Pattern: Don't try to force a design pattern into a situation where it doesn't fit. Applying a pattern inappropriately can make the code more complex and harder to understand.

Start Simple: If a simple solution exists, use it. Don't over-engineer the solution by applying a complex design pattern when a simpler approach will suffice.

Consider the Consequences: Think about the consequences of applying a particular pattern. What are the benefits and drawbacks? How will it affect the code's readability, maintainability, and performance?

Use Patterns as a Communication Tool: Design patterns provide a common vocabulary for developers. Use them to communicate design decisions clearly and effectively.

Study Existing Code: Look for examples of how design patterns have been applied in existing codebases. This can help you understand how to apply them effectively in your own projects.

Example: Choosing Between Strategy and Template Method:

Let's consider a scenario where you need to implement different ways of calculating shipping costs.

Strategy: If the shipping algorithms are completely independent and can be changed at runtime, the Strategy pattern is a good choice. You would define an interface for shipping strategies and create concrete classes for each algorithm (e.g., StandardShipping, ExpressShipping, InternationalShipping). The client can then choose the appropriate strategy at runtime.

Template Method: If the shipping algorithms share a common structure but have some variations in specific steps, the Template Method pattern is more appropriate. You would define an abstract class with a template method that defines the overall structure of the shipping calculation. Subclasses would then implement the specific steps that vary.

Choosing the right pattern depends on the specific requirements and constraints of the system. If the algorithms are highly independent and need to be easily switched, Strategy is the better choice. If they share a common structure, Template Method is more suitable.

Example: Avoiding Overuse of Singleton:

The Singleton pattern is often overused. While it can be useful in certain situations (e.g., managing a database connection), it can also lead to tight coupling and make testing more difficult. Before using Singleton, consider whether a simpler approach, such as dependency injection, might be more appropriate.

The Alchemist's Precision:

Applying design patterns effectively is like an alchemist carefully selecting the right tools and techniques for each stage of the transformation process. By understanding the context, considering the consequences, and choosing the right pattern for the job, you can create more elegant, efficient, and maintainable code, transforming raw code into truly valuable solutions. Remember, design patterns are tools to be used judiciously, not blindly applied.

6.3 Creating Your Own Design Patterns: Capturing and Sharing Knowledge

In our Code Alchemy analogy, creating a design pattern is like discovering a new alchemical formula, a repeatable process for achieving a desired transformation. It's about recognizing a recurring problem, devising a general solution, and documenting it in a way that can be shared and reused by others. This process of capturing and sharing knowledge is crucial for advancing the craft of software development.

When to Create a Design Pattern:

You should consider creating a design pattern when you encounter a recurring problem that:

Has a General Solution: The solution should be applicable to multiple contexts, not just a specific situation.

Has Been Tried and Tested: The solution should have been used successfully in at least three different projects or contexts. This demonstrates that it is a proven and effective approach.

Has a Non-Obvious Solution: The solution should not be immediately obvious. If the solution is straightforward, it doesn't need to be formalized as a design pattern.

Has a Name and Description: The solution should be given a descriptive name and documented clearly so that others can understand and apply it.

The Structure of a Design Pattern:

A well-documented design pattern typically includes the following components:

Pattern Name and Classification: A descriptive name that clearly identifies the pattern (e.g., "Observer," "Factory Method"). The classification categorizes the pattern (creational, structural, or behavioral).

Intent: A brief description of the problem the pattern addresses and the solution it provides.

Motivation: A scenario that illustrates the problem and the context in which the pattern is applicable.

Applicability: Situations in which the pattern can be applied.

Structure: A graphical representation (e.g., a UML class diagram) showing the classes and their relationships.

Participants: A description of the classes and objects involved in the pattern and their responsibilities.

Collaborations: A description of how the participants interact with each other.

Consequences: The benefits and drawbacks of using the pattern, including trade-offs and potential issues.

Implementation: Guidelines for implementing the pattern in a specific programming language.

Sample Code: Code examples demonstrating how to use the pattern.

Known Uses: Examples of real-world applications of the pattern.

Related Patterns: Patterns that are related to or can be used in conjunction with the current pattern.

The Process of Creating a Design Pattern:

Observe Recurring Problems: Pay attention to problems that you encounter repeatedly in your projects.

Develop Solutions: Devise general solutions to these problems.

Refine and Test Solutions: Apply the solutions in different contexts and refine them based on your experience.

Document the Pattern: Document the problem, solution, context, and consequences in a clear and concise manner, following the standard pattern structure.

Share and Review: Share your pattern with other developers and solicit feedback. This helps to validate the pattern and improve its documentation.

Example: A Simple Custom Pattern (Example Purpose Only):

Let's imagine a hypothetical scenario where you frequently need to create objects that require asynchronous initialization. You could create a pattern called "Async Initializer":

Pattern Name: Async Initializer

Intent: Provides a way to create objects that require asynchronous initialization, ensuring that they are fully initialized before being used.

Motivation: Creating objects that rely on asynchronous operations (e.g., network requests, database queries) can lead to race conditions if the objects are used before the initialization is complete.

Structure: (Simplified) An interface `AsyncInitializable` with an `initialize()` method that returns a `Future`. A concrete class implements this interface and performs the asynchronous initialization in the `initialize()` method.

Consequences: Simplifies asynchronous object creation, avoids race conditions, but adds some complexity due to the use of futures.

This is a simplified example, but it illustrates the basic process of creating a design pattern.

The Alchemist's Legacy:

Creating and sharing design patterns is like an alchemist passing on their knowledge and discoveries to future generations. By capturing and documenting proven solutions to common problems, you contribute to the collective wisdom of the software development community and help to elevate the craft of code alchemy. This sharing of knowledge transforms individual insights into lasting and valuable contributions.

Chapter 7

The Alchemist's Forge: Refactoring Techniques

7.1 Extract Method: Isolating Functionality for Better Readability

In the alchemical process of refining code, the "Extract Method" refactoring technique is akin to isolating a specific chemical process in a separate vessel for better control and observation. It involves taking a block of code and extracting it into its own well-named method. This significantly improves code readability, reduces redundancy, and makes the code easier to understand and maintain.

What is Extract Method?

Extract Method is a refactoring technique where you take a block of code within a method and extract it into a new method. The original method then calls the newly extracted method. This process breaks down large, complex methods into smaller, more manageable units of functionality.

Why Use Extract Method?

Improved Readability: Smaller methods are easier to read and understand. They focus on a single, well-defined task, making the code's intent clearer.

Reduced Code Duplication: If the same block of code is used in multiple places, extracting it into a method eliminates the duplication. This reduces the risk of errors and makes it easier to maintain the code.

Increased Code Reusability: Extracted methods can be reused in other parts of the application or even in other projects.

Improved Code Organization: Breaking down large methods into smaller ones improves the overall organization of the code, making it easier to navigate and understand the flow of logic.

Easier Testing: Smaller methods are easier to test because they have a smaller scope and fewer dependencies.

How to Perform Extract Method:

Identify the Code Block: Select the block of code that you want to extract. This should ideally be a logically cohesive unit of functionality.

Create a New Method: Create a new method with a descriptive name that clearly indicates its purpose.

Copy the Code: Copy the selected code block into the new method.

Handle Local Variables: Determine which local variables from the original method are used in the extracted code. Pass these variables as parameters to the new method.

Return Values: If the extracted code produces a result that is used in the original method, return that result from the new method.

Replace the Original Code: Replace the original code block with a call to the new method.

Example:

Let's say you have a method that prints customer details and order information:

Java
```java
void printOrderDetails(Customer customer, Order order) {
    System.out.println("Customer Name: " + customer.getName());
            System.out.println("Customer     Address:     "     +
customer.getAddress());

    System.out.println("Order ID: " + order.getId());
    System.out.println("Order Date: " + order.getDate());
    System.out.println("Order Total: " + order.getTotal());
}
```

You could extract the customer details printing into a separate method:

Java
```java
void printOrderDetails(Customer customer, Order order) {
    printCustomerDetails(customer);

    System.out.println("Order ID: " + order.getId());
    System.out.println("Order Date: " + order.getDate());
    System.out.println("Order Total: " + order.getTotal());
}

void printCustomerDetails(Customer customer) {
    System.out.println("Customer Name: " + customer.getName());
            System.out.println("Customer     Address:     "     +
customer.getAddress());
}
```

And you could further extract the order details printing:

Java
```java
void printOrderDetails(Customer customer, Order order) {
    printCustomerDetails(customer);
```

```
    printOrderInformation(order);
}

void printCustomerDetails(Customer customer) {
    System.out.println("Customer Name: " + customer.getName());
            System.out.println("Customer    Address:    "    +
customer.getAddress());
}

void printOrderInformation(Order order) {
    System.out.println("Order ID: " + order.getId());
    System.out.println("Order Date: " + order.getDate());
    System.out.println("Order Total: " + order.getTotal());
}
```

Now the `printOrderDetails` method is much simpler and easier to understand.

The Alchemist's Separation:

Extract Method is like an alchemist carefully separating different components of a mixture to better understand and work with them. By isolating functionality into well-named methods, you make your code more readable, maintainable, and reusable, transforming complex and unwieldy code into clear and well-structured solutions. This practice is essential for refining code and achieving true elegance in software development.

7.2 Rename   Method/Variable: Improving Clarity and Communication

In the alchemical pursuit of creating understandable and maintainable code, choosing appropriate names for methods and variables is paramount. The "Rename Method/Variable" refactoring technique is akin to giving precise and descriptive labels to the ingredients and apparatus in an alchemist's laboratory. This simple yet powerful technique greatly improves code readability and facilitates communication among developers.

What is Rename Method/Variable?

Rename Method/Variable is a refactoring technique where you change the name of a method or variable to better reflect its purpose or meaning. This seemingly simple change can have a significant impact on code clarity and maintainability.

Why Use Rename Method/Variable?

Improved Readability: Well-chosen names make the code easier to understand and follow. They act as self-documentation, reducing the need for excessive comments.

Enhanced Communication: Clear names facilitate communication among developers. They provide a common vocabulary for discussing the code and its functionality.

Reduced Ambiguity: Ambiguous or misleading names can lead to confusion and errors. Renaming elements to be more precise eliminates this ambiguity.

Easier Maintenance: When code is easy to understand, it's also easier to maintain and modify.

How to Perform Rename Method/Variable:

Identify the Element to Rename: Choose the method or variable that needs a better name.

Choose a Descriptive Name: Select a name that accurately and clearly reflects the element's purpose or meaning. Follow established naming conventions (e.g., camelCase for methods and variables, PascalCase for classes).

Perform the Rename: Use your IDE's refactoring tools to perform the rename. This will automatically update all references to the renamed element throughout the codebase, preventing errors.

Check for Collisions: Ensure that the new name doesn't clash with any existing names in the same scope.

Example:

Let's say you have a method named `getData()` that retrieves user information:

Java
```
List<User> getData() {
    // ... code to retrieve user data
}
```

This name is quite generic. A better name would be `getAllUsers()` or `retrieveUsers()` to be more specific about the data being retrieved.

Similarly, if you have a variable named `t`:

Java
```
int t; // Represents total price
```

This name is very short and doesn't convey much meaning. A better name would be `totalPrice`.

After renaming:

Java
```
List<User> retrieveUsers() {
    // ... code to retrieve user data
}
```

int totalPrice; // Represents total price

The code is now much more readable and understandable.

Best Practices for Naming:

Be Descriptive: Choose names that clearly describe the element's purpose.

Be Concise: Avoid overly long names. Aim for a balance between descriptiveness and conciseness.

Use Consistent Conventions: Follow established naming conventions within your project or organization.

Use Pronounceable Names: Choose names that are easy to pronounce.

Avoid Abbreviations (unless widely understood): Abbreviations can make code cryptic.

Boolean Variables: Use names that clearly indicate a true/false value (e.g., `isLoggedIn`, `hasPermission`).

Method Names: Use verbs to describe the action the method performs (e.g., `calculateTotal()`, `validateInput()`).

Class Names: Use nouns to describe the objects the class represents (e.g., `Customer`, `Order`).

The Alchemist's Precision:

Renaming methods and variables is like an alchemist carefully labeling each ingredient and piece of equipment. Precise and descriptive names improve communication, reduce ambiguity, and make the entire process more efficient. By choosing names that clearly convey meaning, you transform code from a cryptic collection of symbols into a clear and expressive language, facilitating understanding and maintenance. This attention to detail is essential for achieving true elegance in code alchemy.

7.3 Move Method/Field: Organizing Code for Better Cohesion

In the alchemical pursuit of crafting well-structured and maintainable code, the "Move Method/Field" refactoring technique is akin to organizing the tools and ingredients in an alchemist's laboratory for optimal workflow. It involves moving methods and fields to the class where they logically belong, improving cohesion and reducing coupling.

What is Move Method/Field?

Move Method: This refactoring technique involves moving a method from one class to another class where it is more logically related or where it is used more frequently.

Move Field: This technique involves moving a field (instance variable) from one class to another class that uses it more extensively or where it logically belongs.

Why Use Move Method/Field?

Improved Cohesion: Cohesion refers to the degree to which the elements within a class are related to each other. Moving methods and fields to the appropriate class increases cohesion, making each class more focused and easier to understand.

Reduced Coupling: Coupling refers to the degree to which different classes are dependent on each other. Moving methods and fields can reduce coupling by minimizing unnecessary dependencies between classes.

Improved Code Organization: Moving methods and fields to their logical home improves the overall organization of the code, making it easier to navigate and understand the relationships between classes.

Increased Code Reusability: Moving methods to more appropriate classes can make them more reusable in other parts of the application.

How to Perform Move Method/Field:

Move Method:

Determine the Target Class: Identify the class where the method logically belongs or where it is used most frequently.

Copy the Method: Copy the method from the source class to the target class.

Adjust Method Signature (if necessary): If the method uses fields or methods from the source class, you may need to adjust the method signature to accept those values as parameters or make the target class aware of the source class.

Update Callers: Update all calls to the method to point to its new location in the target class.

Remove the Original Method: Remove the original method from the source class.

Move Field:

Determine the Target Class: Identify the class where the field logically belongs or where it is used most extensively.

Move the Field: Move the field from the source class to the target class.

Update Accessors/Mutators (if necessary): If the field had accessors (getters) or mutators (setters), you may need to move or adjust them as well.

Update References: Update all references to the field to point to its new location in the target class.

Example (Move Method):

Let's say you have a Customer class and an Order class:

Java
```java
class Customer {
    // ... customer data

    double calculateOrderTotal(Order order) { // Belongs more logically in Order
        double total = 0;
        for (OrderItem item : order.getItems()) {
            total += item.getPrice() * item.getQuantity();
        }
        return total;
    }
}

class Order {
    List<OrderItem> items;
    // ... other order data
    public List<OrderItem> getItems() { return items;}

}

class OrderItem{
    double price;
    int quantity;
    public double getPrice() {return price;}
```

```java
    public int getQuantity() {return quantity;}
}
```

The `calculateOrderTotal` method is more logically related to the `Order` class, as it operates on order data. You would move it to the `Order` class:

Java
```java
class Customer {
    // ... customer data
}

class Order {
    List<OrderItem> items;
    // ... other order data
    public List<OrderItem> getItems() { return items;}

     double calculateTotal() { //Now it doesn't need to take an order object
        double total = 0;
        for (OrderItem item : items) {
           total += item.getPrice() * item.getQuantity();
        }
        return total;
    }
}
class OrderItem{
    double price;
    int quantity;
    public double getPrice() {return price;}
    public int getQuantity() {return quantity;}
}
```

Now the `Order` class has higher cohesion, as it contains both the order data and the logic for calculating the total. The `Customer` class is no longer unnecessarily coupled to the `Order`'s internal calculations.

The Alchemist's Organization:

Moving methods and fields is like an alchemist carefully organizing the tools and ingredients in their laboratory. By placing elements where they logically belong, you improve the workflow, make it easier to find what you need, and create a more efficient and productive environment. This organizational improvement in code translates to better cohesion, reduced coupling, and ultimately, more maintainable and understandable software.

7.4 Introduce Explaining Variable: Making Code More Self-Documenting

In the alchemical pursuit of creating clear and understandable code, the "Introduce Explaining Variable" refactoring technique is akin to adding clear labels to complex chemical formulas. It involves replacing complex or cryptic expressions with well-named variables, making the code's intent more readily apparent.

What is Introduce Explaining Variable?

Introduce Explaining Variable is a refactoring technique where you replace a complex or hard-to-understand expression with a new variable that has a descriptive name. This variable then holds the result of the expression, making the code easier to read and understand.

Why Use Introduce Explaining Variable?

Improved Readability: Complex expressions can be difficult to decipher at a glance. Introducing well-named variables breaks down these expressions into smaller, more understandable parts.

Increased Clarity: Explaining variables clearly communicate the purpose of intermediate calculations, making the code's intent more obvious.

Simplified Debugging: When debugging, it's easier to inspect the values of named variables than to evaluate complex expressions.

Reduced Complexity: Breaking down complex expressions can reduce the overall cognitive load required to understand the code.

How to Perform Introduce Explaining Variable:

Identify the Complex Expression: Find a complex or hard-to-understand expression within a method.

Declare a New Variable: Declare a new variable with a descriptive name that explains the purpose of the expression.

Assign the Expression to the Variable: Assign the value of the complex expression to the newly declared variable.

Replace the Expression with the Variable: Replace all occurrences of the complex expression with the new variable.

Example:

Let's say you have the following code that calculates the price of an item after applying a discount and tax:

Java
```
double      calculateFinalPrice(double      basePrice,      double
discountPercentage, double taxRate) {
```

```java
    return basePrice * (1 - discountPercentage / 100) * (1 + taxRate
/ 100);
}
```

This expression is a bit difficult to read at first glance. You can introduce explaining variables to make it clearer:

Java
```java
double    calculateFinalPrice(double    basePrice,    double
discountPercentage, double taxRate) {
    double discountFactor = 1 - discountPercentage / 100;
    double priceAfterDiscount = basePrice * discountFactor;
    double taxFactor = 1 + taxRate / 100;
    double finalPrice = priceAfterDiscount * taxFactor;
    return finalPrice;
}
```

Now the code is much easier to understand. The variables `discountFactor`, `priceAfterDiscount`, `taxFactor`, and `finalPrice` clearly explain the steps involved in the calculation.

Another Example (with a more complex condition):

Java
```java
if            ((platform.toUpperCase().contains("MAC")            ||
platform.toUpperCase().contains("LINUX"))                         &&
browser.toUpperCase().equals("CHROME")) {
    // ...
}
```

Introducing explaining variables:

Java

```java
boolean isMacOrLinux = platform.toUpperCase().contains("MAC")
|| platform.toUpperCase().contains("LINUX");
boolean                    isChromeBrowser                    =
browser.toUpperCase().equals("CHROME");

if (isMacOrLinux && isChromeBrowser) {
    // ...
}
```

This is significantly more readable.

When to Use Introduce Explaining Variable:

When you have a complex expression that is difficult to understand.

When an expression is used multiple times in a method.

When an expression involves multiple operations or conditions.

When Not to Use Introduce Explaining Variable:

When the expression is already simple and easy to understand.

When introducing too many variables can clutter the code.

The Alchemist's Labeling:

Introducing explaining variables is like an alchemist carefully labeling each component of a complex formula. These labels make the formula easier to understand, analyze, and reproduce. By using descriptive variable names, you make your code more self-documenting, improving its readability and maintainability, and transforming potentially cryptic code into clear and understandable solutions.

Chapter 8

The Alchemist's Workshop: Tools and Technologies

8.1 Leveraging IDEs: Utilizing Refactoring Features and Code Analysis Tools

In the alchemical pursuit of crafting high-quality code, Integrated Development Environments (IDEs) are the modern alchemist's most powerful tools. They provide a rich set of features that streamline the refactoring process, automate tedious tasks, and help identify potential problems in the code. Leveraging these features effectively is crucial for maximizing productivity and achieving code excellence.

Refactoring Features:

Modern IDEs offer a wide range of automated refactoring features that make it much easier and safer to restructure code. These features handle the tedious and error-prone aspects of refactoring, ensuring that all necessary changes are made consistently throughout the codebase. Some common refactoring features include:

Rename: Automatically renames variables, methods, classes, and other code elements, updating all references throughout the project. This prevents errors caused by manually renaming elements.

Extract Method: Automatically extracts a block of code into a new method, handling parameter passing and return values.

Extract Variable/Constant: Creates a new variable or constant from an expression, making the code more readable.

Inline Method/Variable: Replaces a method call or variable usage with its actual code or value.

Move Method/Field: Moves a method or field to another class, updating all references.

Pull Up/Push Down: Moves methods or fields up or down the inheritance hierarchy.

Change Signature: Changes the signature of a method (e.g., adding, removing, or reordering parameters), updating all calls to the method.

Extract Interface/Superclass: Creates a new interface or superclass from an existing class.

Introduce Parameter Object: Creates a new class to encapsulate related parameters, reducing the number of arguments passed to a method.

Safe Delete: Safely deletes code elements, checking for usages before deletion to prevent errors.

Using IDE Refactoring Features:

To use these features effectively:

Select the Code: Select the code you want to refactor (e.g., a block of code to extract into a method, a variable to rename).

Use the Refactoring Menu/Shortcut: Access the refactoring menu (usually through a right-click context menu or a keyboard shortcut) and choose the appropriate refactoring.

Preview and Apply: Most IDEs allow you to preview the changes before applying them, giving you a chance to verify that the refactoring is being done correctly.

Code Analysis Tools:

IDEs also provide powerful code analysis tools that can help identify potential problems in the code, such as:

Static Analysis: Analyzes the code without executing it, looking for potential errors, code smells, and style violations. Examples include:

FindBugs/SpotBugs (Java): Detects bug patterns in Java code.

PMD (Java): Finds common programming flaws like unused variables, empty catch blocks, and overly complex expressions.

Checkstyle (Java): Enforces coding style conventions.

ESLint (JavaScript): Identifies and reports on stylistic issues and potential errors in JavaScript code.

Many IDEs have their own built-in static analysis tools.

Code Inspections: Similar to static analysis, but often more integrated into the IDE and providing more specific suggestions.

Code Metrics: Measures various aspects of the code, such as cyclomatic complexity, lines of code, and coupling. These metrics can help identify areas of the code that are overly complex or tightly coupled.

Using Code Analysis Tools:

Configure Rules: Configure the rules and settings of the code analysis tools to match your project's coding standards and requirements.

Run Analysis Regularly: Run the code analysis tools regularly to identify potential problems early in the development process.

Address Issues: Address the issues reported by the code analysis tools to improve code quality.

Example (IntelliJ IDEA):

In IntelliJ IDEA, you can use the "Refactor This" menu (usually accessed with `Ctrl+Alt+Shift+T` or `Cmd+Alt+Shift+T`) to access a wide range of refactoring options. You can also use the "Analyze" menu to run code inspections and other analysis tools.

The Alchemist's Toolkit:

IDEs are the modern alchemist's toolkit, providing powerful tools for refining and improving code. By leveraging the refactoring features and code analysis tools available in IDEs, you can significantly improve your productivity, write higher-quality code, and transform raw code into truly valuable solutions. These tools automate tedious tasks, prevent errors, and provide valuable insights into the code, making the refactoring process more efficient and effective.

8.2 Version Control Systems: Tracking Changes and Experimenting Safely

In the alchemical pursuit of creating and refining code, Version Control Systems (VCS) are like the meticulous laboratory notebooks of the modern alchemist. They provide a comprehensive history of all changes made to the codebase, allowing developers to track progress, revert to previous states, and experiment with new ideas without fear of losing work.

What is a Version Control System?

A Version Control System is a software tool that tracks changes to files over time. It allows you to:

Track Changes: Record every modification made to the codebase, including who made the change, when it was made, and what was changed.

Revert to Previous Versions: Go back to earlier versions of the code if necessary.

Branch and Merge: Create separate branches of the code to work on different features or bug fixes in isolation, and then merge those changes back into the main codebase.

Collaborate Effectively: Facilitate collaboration among multiple developers by managing conflicts and ensuring that everyone is working with the latest version of the code.

Why are VCS Important for Refactoring and Experimentation?

Safe Experimentation: VCS allows you to create branches to experiment with new ideas or refactoring approaches without affecting the main codebase. If the experiment is successful, you can merge the changes back in. If it's not, you can simply discard the branch.

Undo Changes: If you make a mistake during refactoring or introduce a bug, you can easily revert to a previous version of the code.

Track Refactoring Progress: VCS provides a history of all refactoring changes, making it easier to track progress and understand the evolution of the code.

Facilitate Code Reviews: VCS makes code reviews easier by showing exactly what changes have been made.

Collaboration: VCS is essential for team-based development, allowing multiple developers to work on the same codebase simultaneously without overwriting each other's changes.

Common Version Control Systems:

Git: The most popular VCS today. It's a distributed VCS, meaning that each developer has a full copy of the repository on their local machine.

Subversion (SVN): A centralized VCS, where all changes are stored in a central repository.

Mercurial (Hg): Another distributed VCS, similar to Git.

Key Concepts in Git (as the most common VCS):

Repository (Repo): A collection of files and their history.

Commit: A snapshot of the changes made to the code at a specific point in time.

Branch: A separate line of development.

Merge: Combining changes from one branch into another.

Pull: Downloading changes from a remote repository.

Push: Uploading changes to a remote repository.

Example (Basic Git Workflow):

Create a Branch: `git checkout -b feature/new-feature` (creates a new branch named "feature/new-feature")

Make Changes: Make your code changes, including refactoring.

Commit Changes: `git add .` (stages all changes), then `git commit -m "Refactor: extracted method for calculating total"` (commits the changes with a descriptive message).

Test Changes: Run your unit tests to ensure that your changes haven't introduced any bugs.

Merge Changes: `git checkout main` (switches back to the main branch), then `git merge feature/new-feature`(merges the changes from the feature branch into the main branch).

The Alchemist's Logbook:

Version Control Systems are the alchemist's logbook, meticulously recording every experiment and observation. They provide a safety net for experimentation, allowing you to try new approaches without fear of losing work. By using VCS effectively, you can track the evolution of your code, collaborate efficiently with other developers, and transform raw code into refined and valuable solutions with greater confidence. They are an indispensable tool for any serious software developer.

8.3 Continuous Integration and Continuous Delivery: Automating the Refactoring Process

In the alchemical pursuit of creating and maintaining high-quality code, Continuous Integration (CI) and Continuous Delivery (CD) are like automated refining processes. They establish a pipeline that automatically builds, tests, and deploys code changes, ensuring that refactoring efforts are integrated smoothly and potential issues are identified early.

What is Continuous Integration (CI)?

Continuous Integration is a development practice that requires developers to integrate code into a shared repository[1]frequently, preferably several times a day. Each integration is then verified by an automated build and[2] test process.

Key Practices of CI:

Frequent Integration: Developers commit their code changes to a shared repository regularly.

Automated Build: Every commit triggers an automated build process that compiles the code and creates executable artifacts.

Automated Testing: Automated tests (unit tests, integration tests, etc.) are run as part of the build process to verify the correctness of the code.

Fast Feedback: Developers receive immediate feedback on the success or failure of the build and tests.

What is Continuous Delivery (CD)?

Continuous Delivery extends CI by automating the release process. It ensures that code changes can be released to production at any time.

Key Practices of CD:

Automated Deployment: Deployments to various environments (e.g., development, testing, staging, production) are automated.

Release Orchestration: The process of coordinating and managing releases is automated.

Infrastructure as Code: Infrastructure is managed and provisioned through code, enabling automation and repeatability.

Continuous Monitoring: The application and infrastructure are continuously monitored to detect and address issues quickly.

How CI/CD Enhances Refactoring:

Early Detection of Errors: CI/CD catches errors introduced during refactoring much earlier in the development process. If a refactoring change breaks existing functionality, the automated tests will fail, providing immediate feedback to the developer.

Increased Confidence: CI/CD provides confidence to make refactoring changes. Knowing that changes will be automatically tested reduces the fear of introducing regressions.

Faster Feedback Loop: The automated build and test process provides a much faster feedback loop than manual testing. This allows developers to iterate more quickly and make more frequent refactoring changes.

Automated Regression Testing: Every commit triggers a full suite of tests, ensuring that no existing functionality is broken by refactoring changes.

Simplified Integration: CI/CD makes it easier to integrate refactoring changes from multiple developers working on the same codebase.

Reduced Risk of Large Refactorings: By encouraging small, frequent refactorings integrated continuously, CI/CD reduces the need for large, risky refactoring projects.

Example CI/CD Workflow with Refactoring:

A developer creates a new branch for a refactoring task.

The developer makes small, incremental refactoring changes.

After each small change, the developer commits the changes and pushes them to the remote repository.

The CI server detects the new commit and automatically triggers a build.

The build process compiles the code and runs all automated tests.

If all tests pass, the build is considered successful.

If any tests fail, the CI server notifies the developer, who can then fix the issue.

Once the refactoring is complete and all tests pass, the developer creates a pull request to merge the changes into the main branch.

After code review, the pull request is merged.

The merge to the main branch triggers a deployment to a staging or production environment (depending on the CD setup).

Tools for CI/CD:

Jenkins: A popular open-source CI server.

GitLab CI/CD: Integrated CI/CD features within GitLab.

GitHub Actions: CI/CD features integrated within GitHub.

Azure DevOps: A cloud-based DevOps platform.

CircleCI: A cloud-based CI/CD platform.

The Alchemist's Automated Refinery:

CI/CD is the alchemist's automated refinery, continuously purifying and improving the code. By automating the build, test, and deployment processes, CI/CD ensures that refactoring efforts are integrated smoothly and potential issues are identified early. This continuous refinement leads to higher-quality code, faster development cycles, and more reliable software.

Chapter 9

The Alchemist's Journey: A Case Study

9.1 Analyzing a Real-World Codebase: Identifying Areas for Improvement

In our Code Alchemy analogy, analyzing a real-world codebase is like examining a raw ore sample. The goal is to identify impurities (code smells, design flaws, performance bottlenecks) that prevent it from reaching its full potential. This analysis is the first step towards refining the codebase and transforming it into a more valuable asset.

Steps for Analyzing a Codebase:

Understand the Purpose and Context: Before diving into the code, understand the application's purpose, domain, and target users. This context will help you evaluate the code's design and functionality.

Start with High-Level Architecture: Get a high-level overview of the codebase's architecture. Identify the main components, their relationships, and the overall structure. This can often be done through documentation, diagrams, or by exploring the project's directory structure.

Identify Code Smells: Look for common code smells, which are indicators of potential problems. Some common smells include:

Long Methods/Classes: Methods or classes that are excessively long and complex.

Duplicated Code: Identical or very similar code blocks repeated in multiple places.

Large Parameter Lists: Methods with too many parameters.

Data Clumps: Groups of data that frequently appear together.

Primitive Obsession: Excessive use of primitive data types instead of creating meaningful objects.

Switch Statements/Chains of If-Else: Complex conditional logic that can be simplified using polymorphism or other techniques.

Feature Envy: A method in one class that seems more interested in the data of another class.

God Classes: Classes that know and do too much.

Analyze Dependencies: Examine the dependencies between different parts of the code. Look for tight coupling, which can make the code difficult to change and maintain.

Review Code Style and Conventions: Check if the code follows consistent coding style conventions. Inconsistent style can make the code harder to read and understand.

Evaluate Test Coverage: Assess the quality and extent of the test suite. Look for areas with low test coverage, which may indicate higher risk of bugs.

Consider Performance: If performance is a critical concern, use profiling tools to identify performance bottlenecks.

Use Static Analysis Tools: Use static analysis tools (like FindBugs, PMD, Checkstyle, ESLint) to automatically detect potential problems in the code.

Look for Security Vulnerabilities: If the application handles sensitive data, perform a security audit to identify potential vulnerabilities.

Tools for Code Analysis:

IDEs (Integrated Development Environments): Most IDEs have built-in code inspection and analysis features.

Static Analysis Tools: FindBugs/SpotBugs, PMD, Checkstyle (Java), ESLint (JavaScript), SonarQube.

Code Metrics Tools: Tools that measure code complexity, lines of code, and other metrics.

Profiling Tools: Tools that help identify performance bottlenecks.

Example: Identifying Areas for Improvement:

Let's imagine you are analyzing a codebase with the following method:

Java
```
public void processUserData(String name, String address, String phone, String email, int age, boolean isActive, String country, String city, String zipCode) {
    // ... many lines of code that use all these parameters
    if (country.equals("US")) {
        // ... US specific logic
    } else if (country.equals("CA")) {
        // ... Canada specific logic
    }
    // ... more code
}
```

Here are some potential areas for improvement:

Large Parameter List: The method has too many parameters. This can be addressed by creating a `User` object or a `UserAddress` object to encapsulate related data.

Switch Statement/Chains of If-Else: The conditional logic based on the `country` could be simplified using polymorphism or a strategy pattern.

Long Method: The method is likely too long and should be broken down into smaller, more focused methods.

The Alchemist's Examination:

Analyzing a codebase is like an alchemist carefully examining a sample of ore, looking for clues about its composition and potential value. By identifying code smells, analyzing dependencies, and using appropriate tools, you can pinpoint areas for improvement and begin the process of refining the codebase. This analysis is the crucial first step in transforming raw code into a valuable and well-structured application.

9.2 Applying Refactoring Techniques: Step-by-Step Transformation

In our Code Alchemy analogy, applying refactoring techniques is like performing a chemical transformation in a controlled and methodical way. Each step must be carefully planned and executed to achieve the desired result without unintended side effects. This step-by-step approach ensures that the refactoring process is safe, predictable, and ultimately successful.

The Refactoring Process: A Step-by-Step Guide

Identify the Area for Improvement: Use the analysis techniques discussed earlier to pinpoint specific areas of the codebase that need refactoring. This could be a long method, duplicated code, a complex conditional statement, or any other code smell.

Ensure Adequate Test Coverage: Before starting any refactoring, make sure you have sufficient test coverage for the code you are about to change. This is crucial for preventing regressions. Write new tests if necessary.

Choose the Appropriate Refactoring Technique(s): Select the refactoring technique(s) that are most appropriate for addressing the identified problem. Some common techniques include:

Extract Method: To break down long methods into smaller, more manageable units.

Rename Method/Variable: To improve code clarity and communication.

Move Method/Field: To improve code organization and cohesion.

Introduce Explaining Variable: To make complex expressions more understandable.

Extract Class: To create new classes to encapsulate related data and behavior.

Replace Conditional with Polymorphism: To simplify complex conditional logic.

Make Small, Incremental Changes: Refactor in small, incremental steps. This makes it easier to track changes and identify any problems that may arise. Avoid making large, sweeping changes all at once.

Test After Each Change: After each small change, run your unit tests to ensure that you haven't broken anything. If a test fails, revert the change and try a different approach.

Commit Frequently: Commit your changes to version control frequently. This creates checkpoints that you can revert to if necessary.

Review and Iterate: After completing a refactoring task, review the changes with your team and iterate on the code as needed.

Example: Refactoring a Long Method:

Let's revisit the `processUserData` method from the previous example:

Java
```java
public void processUserData(String name, String address, String phone, String email, int age, boolean isActive, String country, String city, String zipCode) {
    // ... many lines of code that use all these parameters
    if (country.equals("US")) {
        // ... US specific logic
    } else if (country.equals("CA")) {
        // ... Canada specific logic
    }
    // ... more code
}
```

Here's a step-by-step refactoring approach:

Identify the Problem: The method is too long and has too many parameters.

Ensure Adequate Test Coverage: Write unit tests that cover the different scenarios handled by the method (e.g., US user, Canada user, other users).

Choose Refactoring Techniques:

Extract Class: Create a User class to encapsulate the user data.

Extract Method: Extract the country-specific logic into separate methods.

Make Small Changes and Test:

Step 1: Extract User class:

Java

```java
class User {
    String name;
    String address;
    String phone;
    String email;
    int age;
    boolean isActive;
    String country;
    String city;
    String zipCode;
    // ... constructor, getters, setters
}
```

```java
public void processUserData(User user) {
    // ... use user object instead of individual parameters
    if (user.country.equals("US")) {
        // ... US specific logic
    } else if (user.country.equals("CA")) {
        // ... Canada specific logic
    }
    // ... more code
}
```

Run tests.
Step 2: Extract country-specific logic:

Java

```java
public void processUserData(User user) {
    if (user.country.equals("US")) {
        processUSUser(user);
    } else if (user.country.equals("CA")) {
        processCAUser(user);
    }
    // ... more code
}

private void processUSUser(User user) {
    // ... US specific logic
}

private void processCAUser(User user) {
    // ... Canada specific logic
}
```

Run tests.

Commit Frequently: Commit after each step.

Review and Iterate: Review the changes and make further adjustments if needed.

The Alchemist's Precision:

Applying refactoring techniques step-by-step is like an alchemist carefully controlling each stage of a chemical reaction. By making small, incremental changes and testing after each step, you can ensure that the transformation is successful and that the resulting code is cleaner, more maintainable, and more valuable. This methodical approach is essential for achieving true mastery of code alchemy.

9.3 Measuring the Impact: Evaluating the Benefits of Refactoring

In our Code Alchemy analogy, measuring the impact of refactoring is like analyzing the purity and properties of the refined substance. It's about demonstrating the tangible benefits of the transformation and justifying the time and effort invested.

What to Measure:

The impact of refactoring can be measured in several ways, depending on the specific goals of the refactoring effort. Some key metrics to consider include:

Code Complexity: Refactoring often aims to reduce code complexity. This can be measured using metrics like:

Cyclomatic Complexity: Measures the number of independent paths through the code. Lower cyclomatic complexity indicates simpler code.

Lines of Code (LOC): While not always a direct indicator of complexity, a significant reduction in LOC after refactoring can suggest improved code conciseness.

Code Churn: Measures the frequency of changes to the code. Refactoring can sometimes lead to an initial increase in churn as the code is restructured, but ideally, it should lead to a decrease in churn over the long term, as the code becomes easier to maintain.

Test Coverage: Refactoring often involves improving test coverage. Measure the percentage of code covered by unit tests before and after refactoring.

Bug Rate: Track the number of bugs reported in the refactored code. A successful refactoring effort should lead to a decrease in the bug rate.

Development Time: Measure the time it takes to implement new features or fix bugs in the refactored code. Refactoring should ideally lead to faster development times.

Code Readability: While harder to quantify, code readability is a crucial aspect. This can be assessed through code reviews, asking developers to rate the readability of the code before and after refactoring.

Maintainability: Similar to readability, maintainability can be assessed through surveys or by tracking the time it takes to make changes to the code.

Performance (If Applicable): If the refactoring aimed to improve performance, measure relevant performance metrics (e.g., execution time, memory usage) before and after refactoring.

How to Measure:

Code Analysis Tools: Tools like SonarQube, PMD, and Checkstyle can provide metrics like cyclomatic complexity, lines of code, and code style violations.

Test Coverage Tools: Tools like JaCoCo (Java) and Coverage.py (Python) can measure test coverage.

Version Control System (VCS): VCS tools like Git can be used to track code churn and identify changes made during refactoring.

Issue Tracking Systems: Issue tracking systems like Jira can be used to track bug reports and development time.

Code Reviews: Conduct code reviews to assess code readability and maintainability.

Surveys and Feedback: Gather feedback from developers on the impact of refactoring.

Example: Measuring the Impact of Extract Method:

Let's say you refactor a long method by extracting several smaller methods. You could measure the following:

Cyclomatic Complexity: Measure the cyclomatic complexity of the original method and the extracted methods. You should see a decrease in the overall cyclomatic complexity.

Lines of Code: Compare the total lines of code before and after refactoring. The total LOC might increase slightly due to the new method definitions, but the individual methods will be shorter and easier to understand.

Testability: Evaluate how easy it is to write unit tests for the original method compared to the extracted methods. The extracted methods should be easier to test due to their smaller scope.

Example: Measuring the Impact of Replacing Conditional with Polymorphism:

If you refactor a complex `switch` statement or `if-else` chain using polymorphism, you could measure:

Code Complexity: The code should become less complex and easier to understand.

Extensibility: It should become easier to add new cases or behaviors without modifying existing code.

Presenting the Results:

When presenting the results of your refactoring efforts, focus on the tangible benefits. Use charts, graphs, and clear explanations to demonstrate the impact of the changes. For example:

"Refactoring reduced the average cyclomatic complexity of our core components by 30%."

"Test coverage increased from 70% to 95% after refactoring."

"The time to implement new features in the refactored module decreased by 20%."

The Alchemist's Assay:

Measuring the impact of refactoring is like an alchemist performing an assay to determine the purity and value of the refined substance. By using appropriate metrics and tools, you can demonstrate the tangible benefits of your refactoring efforts and justify the investment in code quality. This data-driven approach helps to solidify refactoring as a valuable and essential practice in software development.

Chapter 10

The Alchemist's Legacy: Maintaining and Evolving Code

10.1 Building a Sustainable Codebase: Cultivating a Culture of Continuous Improvement

Let's discuss the importance of cultivating a culture of continuous improvement to build and maintain a sustainable codebase:

Building a Sustainable Codebase: Cultivating a Culture of Continuous Improvement

In our Code Alchemy analogy, building a sustainable codebase is like establishing a thriving alchemical tradition, where knowledge is passed down, techniques are refined, and the pursuit of excellence is a continuous endeavor. It's not a one-time transformation but an ongoing process of improvement, adaptation, and growth.

What is a Sustainable Codebase?

A sustainable codebase is one that is:

Maintainable: Easy to understand, modify, and extend.

Scalable: Able to handle increasing demands and complexity.

Reliable: Free of bugs and performs as expected.

Adaptable: Able to adapt to changing requirements and technologies.

Understandable: Well-documented and easy for developers to work with.

Cultivating a Culture of Continuous Improvement:

Building a sustainable codebase requires a culture of continuous improvement, where everyone on the team is committed to writing high-quality code and constantly seeking ways to improve it. Here are some key practices for fostering such a culture:

Embrace Refactoring as a Regular Practice: Refactoring should not be a one-time event but an ongoing process integrated into the development workflow. Encourage small, frequent refactorings as part of every development task.

Promote Code Reviews: Regular code reviews are essential for identifying code smells, sharing knowledge, and ensuring code quality. Make code reviews a constructive and collaborative process.

Encourage Test-Driven Development (TDD): TDD helps to write more testable and well-designed code from the beginning. Encourage the practice of writing tests before writing code.

Invest in Automation: Automate as much of the development process as possible, including building, testing, and deployment. This frees up developers to focus on more important tasks and reduces the risk of human error.

Establish Coding Standards and Guidelines: Define clear coding standards and guidelines to ensure consistency across the codebase. Use static analysis tools to enforce these standards automatically.

Prioritize Technical Debt Management: Track and manage technical debt proactively. Address small pieces of technical debt regularly to prevent it from accumulating and becoming a major problem.

Foster a Learning Environment: Encourage continuous learning and knowledge sharing within the team. Provide opportunities for developers to learn new techniques and best practices.

Celebrate Successes: Recognize and celebrate successes in improving code quality. This reinforces the importance of continuous improvement and motivates the team.

Promote Ownership and Accountability: Encourage developers to take ownership of the code they write and be accountable for its quality.

Regularly Review and Adapt: Regularly review your processes and practices and adapt them as needed. The best approach to building a sustainable codebase will evolve over time.

Key Principles for Sustainable Code:

Keep it Simple, Stupid (KISS): Avoid unnecessary complexity. Aim for simple and straightforward solutions.

You Ain't Gonna Need It (YAGNI): Don't add functionality that you don't need right now. Focus on implementing what is required for the current task.

Don't Repeat Yourself (DRY): Avoid code duplication. Extract common logic into reusable methods or components.

Principle of Least Astonishment (POLA): Code should behave in a way that is consistent with users' expectations.

The Alchemist's Legacy:

Building a sustainable codebase is like establishing a lasting alchemical legacy. It's about creating a tradition of excellence, where knowledge is shared, techniques are refined, and the pursuit of improvement is a continuous journey. By fostering a culture of continuous improvement, you create a codebase that is not only functional but also adaptable, maintainable, and valuable for years to come. This is the ultimate goal of Code Alchemy: to transform raw code into a lasting and valuable asset.

10.2 The Value of Refactoring: Investing in the Future of Your Software

In our Code Alchemy analogy, refactoring is not just about cleaning up code; it's about transforming base metals into gold. It's an investment in the future of your software, ensuring that it remains valuable, adaptable, and maintainable over time. Refactoring is not an expense; it's a strategic investment that pays dividends in the long run.

Recap of Refactoring Benefits:

Improved Readability: Refactored code is easier to understand, making it easier for developers to work with and maintain. This reduces the time and effort required for future development and maintenance tasks.

Reduced Complexity: Refactoring simplifies complex code, making it less prone to errors and easier to modify. This reduces the risk of introducing bugs and makes it easier to implement new features.

Improved Maintainability: Cleaner code is easier to maintain and modify in the future. This reduces maintenance costs and extends the lifespan of the software.

Improved Performance (Sometimes): While not the primary goal, refactoring can sometimes lead to performance improvements by optimizing algorithms or data structures.

Improved Design: Refactoring improves the overall design of the code, making it more modular, cohesive, and extensible. This makes it easier to adapt the software to changing requirements and technologies.

Reduced Technical Debt: Refactoring helps to address technical debt, which is the implied cost of rework caused by choosing an easy solution now instead of a better approach that would take longer. By reducing technical debt, you reduce the long-term costs of maintaining the software.

Increased Agility: Refactored code is easier to change, which makes it easier to respond to changing market demands and customer needs. This increases the agility of the development team.

Enhanced Collaboration: Cleaner, more understandable code facilitates better communication and collaboration among developers.

Increased Developer Satisfaction: Working with clean, well-structured code is more enjoyable and rewarding for developers. This can lead to increased job satisfaction and reduced turnover.

Refactoring as an Investment:

Viewing refactoring as an investment rather than an expense is a crucial mindset shift. While refactoring does require an upfront investment of time and effort, it yields significant returns over the long term.

Short-Term Costs, Long-Term Gains: Refactoring might seem like it slows down development in the short term, but it significantly reduces development and maintenance costs in the long term.

Preventing Future Problems: Refactoring proactively addresses potential problems before they become major issues. This prevents costly rework and delays in the future.

Enabling Future Growth: Refactored code is more adaptable and extensible, which enables the software to grow and evolve over time.

When to Refactor:

Before Adding New Features: Refactoring before adding new features can make the implementation easier and reduce the risk of introducing bugs.

During Bug Fixing: When fixing a bug, take the opportunity to refactor the surrounding code to prevent similar bugs from occurring in the future.

During Code Reviews: Code reviews are a great opportunity to identify areas for refactoring.

When Code Smells are Detected: When you encounter code smells, it's a sign that refactoring is needed.

Regularly, as Part of the Development Process: Refactoring should be an ongoing activity, not a one-time event.

The Alchemist's Masterpiece:

Refactoring is the alchemist's final refinement, transforming raw code into a masterpiece of engineering. It's an investment in the future of your software, ensuring that it remains valuable, adaptable, and maintainable for years to come. By embracing refactoring as a core practice, you create software that not only meets current needs but also lays a strong foundation for future growth and innovation. This is the true culmination of Code Alchemy: creating software that stands the test of time.

10.3 Becoming a Code Alchemist: Mastering the Art of Transformation

Our exploration of Code Alchemy has revealed that writing and maintaining high-quality code is not just a technical skill; it's an art. It's about transforming raw, functional code into elegant, maintainable, and valuable solutions. This transformation requires a combination of technical knowledge, disciplined practices, and a commitment to continuous improvement.

Key Principles of Code Alchemy:

Understanding the Fundamentals: A solid understanding of programming principles, data structures, and algorithms is essential. This is the foundation upon which all code transformations are built.

Identifying Code Smells: Developing a keen eye for code smells is crucial for recognizing areas that need improvement. These "impurities" hinder readability, maintainability, and scalability.

Mastering Refactoring Techniques: Refactoring is the core process of code transformation. Mastering various refactoring techniques allows you to make changes safely and effectively.

Embracing Test-Driven Development (TDD): TDD helps to write more testable and well-designed code from the start, making refactoring easier and safer.

Leveraging IDEs and Tools: Modern IDEs and code analysis tools provide powerful support for refactoring and code quality improvement.

Using Version Control Systems (VCS): VCS is essential for tracking changes, experimenting safely, and collaborating effectively.

Implementing Continuous Integration and Continuous Delivery (CI/CD): CI/CD automates the build, test, and deployment processes, ensuring that refactoring efforts are integrated smoothly.

Applying Design Patterns Effectively: Design patterns provide proven solutions to recurring design problems, promoting code reuse and improving design quality.

Writing Meaningful Comments: Comments should explain the "why" behind the code, not just the "what."

Measuring the Impact of Refactoring: Tracking key metrics helps to demonstrate the tangible benefits of refactoring efforts.

Cultivating a Culture of Continuous Improvement: A commitment to continuous improvement is essential for building and maintaining a sustainable codebase.

The Path to Mastery:

Becoming a true Code Alchemist is a journey that requires continuous learning, practice, and dedication. Here are some steps you can take to further your mastery:

Practice Refactoring Regularly: The more you refactor, the better you will become at it. Start with small refactorings and gradually work your way up to more complex transformations.

Study Design Patterns: Learn the common design patterns and practice applying them in different contexts.

Read Code from Experienced Developers: Studying well-written code can provide valuable insights into good coding practices and refactoring techniques.

Participate in Code Reviews: Code reviews provide an excellent opportunity to learn from others and receive feedback on your own code.

Contribute to Open Source Projects: Contributing to open source projects can expose you to different coding styles and refactoring approaches.

Stay Up-to-Date with New Technologies and Best Practices: The field of software development is constantly evolving. Stay current with new technologies and best practices to keep your skills sharp.

The Alchemist's Transformation:

Just as the alchemists of old sought to transform base metals into gold, we as Code Alchemists strive to transform raw code into valuable and enduring software. This transformation is not just about writing functional code; it's about crafting code that is elegant, maintainable, and adaptable. It's about creating software that not only solves problems today but also lays a strong foundation for future innovation.

By embracing the principles and practices of Code Alchemy, you embark on a path of continuous improvement, transforming yourself into a true master of code transformation. The journey is ongoing, but the rewards are well worth the effort: the creation of software that is truly a work of art.